THE HUMAN BODY

THE RESPIRATORY SYSTEM

By John M. Shea, MD

Gareth Stevens
Publishing

Please visit our website, www.garethstevens.com. For a free color catalog of all our high-quality books, call toll free 1-800-542-2595 or fax 1-877-542-2596.

Library of Congress Cataloging-in-Publication Data

Shea, John M.
The respiratory system / John M. Shea.
   p. cm. — (The human body)
Includes index.
ISBN 978-1-4339-6594-4 (pbk.)
ISBN 978-1-4339-6595-1 (6-pack)
ISBN 978-1-4339-6592-0 (library binding)
1. Respiratory system—Juvenile literature. I. Title.
QP145.S44 2012b
612.2—dc23

                  2011036121

First Edition

Published in 2012 by
Gareth Stevens Publishing
111 East 14th Street, Suite 349
New York, NY 10003

Copyright © 2012 Gareth Stevens Publishing

Designer: Daniel Hosek
Editor: Greg Roza

Photo credits: Cover, p. 1 Thinkstock.com; all backgrounds, pp. 5, 7 (all images), 11 (all images), 13 (lungs, RBCs), 15, 17, 19 (all images), 20, 21, 25, 27, 28, 29 Shutterstock.com; pp. 8–9, 13 (alveoli) 3D Clinic/Getty Images; p. 23 Ralph Hutchins/ Visuals Unlimited/Getty Images.

Printed in the United States of America

CPSIA compliance information: Batch #CW12GS: For further information contact Gareth Stevens, New York, New York at 1-800-542-2595.

Contents

Words in the glossary appear in **bold** type
the first time they are used in the text.

The Respiratory System

Breathing is a familiar action for everyone. We breathe to bring fresh, oxygen-rich air into our bodies. Even at rest, our bodies constantly need oxygen to help turn food into energy. Our lungs fill with air when we inhale, or breathe in. When we exhale, or breathe out, we release stale air containing carbon dioxide back into the environment. This happens about 15 times a minute, or over 20,000 times a day!

The respiratory system is composed of an important group of organs that tirelessly make sure your body has a sufficient supply of oxygen to meet its needs. At the same time, the respiratory system makes sure your body eliminates carbon dioxide before high levels of this gas can cause harm.

IN THE FLESH

The world record for holding one's breath is over 19 minutes! Most of us, however, can't hold our breath for more than 2 minutes.

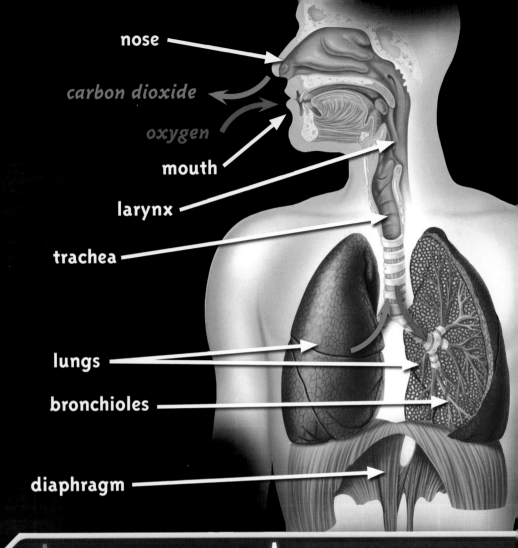

nose

carbon dioxide

oxygen

mouth

larynx

trachea

lungs

bronchioles

diaphragm

IN THE AIR

We can't see, smell, or taste air. But it's vital for survival. About 21 percent of air is made up of the gas oxygen, which our bodies use to produce energy from food. Nitrogen gas makes up 78 percent. The remaining 1 percent contains small amounts of gases such as helium, methane, and water vapor. Carbon dioxide gas makes up only 0.03 percent of air. Most scientists think that even a small increase in carbon dioxide can make temperatures on Earth hotter.

5

Oxygen and Carbon Dioxide

Most life on Earth needs oxygen to stay alive. Animals need oxygen to transform foods, such as sugar and fat, into energy. For **bacteria** and other very small **organisms**, oxygen simply crosses **cell membranes** to get where it's needed. For larger animals, such as humans, a **circulatory system** delivers oxygen throughout the body. The job of the respiratory system is to provide the circulatory system with a continuous supply of oxygen.

When cells use oxygen and sugar to make energy, carbon dioxide is produced as waste. Too much carbon dioxide can be poisonous to animals. So, another job of the circulatory system is to help move carbon dioxide from the cells to the lungs, where it's exhaled and removed from the body.

IN THE FLESH

Fire is a nonliving thing that uses oxygen and creates carbon dioxide. It needs oxygen to burn. Burning wood produces carbon dioxide.

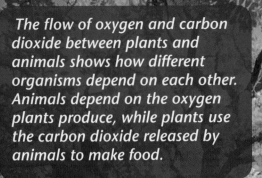

The flow of oxygen and carbon dioxide between plants and animals shows how different organisms depend on each other. Animals depend on the oxygen plants produce, while plants use the carbon dioxide released by animals to make food.

oxygen

carbon dioxide from animals

PHOTOSYNTHESIS

Plants play a vital role in our environment. During photosynthesis, plants use energy from sunlight to change carbon dioxide into sugar. In doing so, plants produce oxygen as a waste product and release it into the air. Plants not only provide food for us to eat, but they help keep our air clean and fresh as well.

The Upper Respiratory Tract

Getting oxygen into the body requires air entering through the mouth and nose. Although we sometimes breathe through our mouths (for example, when we're talking), we most often breathe through our noses. There's a good reason for this. The inside of your nose is lined with many tiny hairs and a layer of **mucus**. These act as a filter that prevents dust, bacteria, and other dangerous microscopic particles from traveling deep into your lungs where they may cause illness or injury.

The mouth and the nasal passage join in an area called the pharynx, or throat. At the bottom of the throat is a flap of **cartilage** called the epiglottis. It guards the beginning of the trachea (or "windpipe") from food that has been swallowed.

IN THE FLESH

The body tries to clear dust and other particles filtered by the nose by exhaling very forcefully: a sneeze!

SENSE OF SMELL

Every time we inhale, air flows over many specialized cells in our nose called odor receptors. These cells are very sensitive to many different chemicals in the air and can recognize over 10,000 unique odors! Our sense of smell can act as an early warning for danger, such as the smell of smoke or the odor of rotten food before we eat.

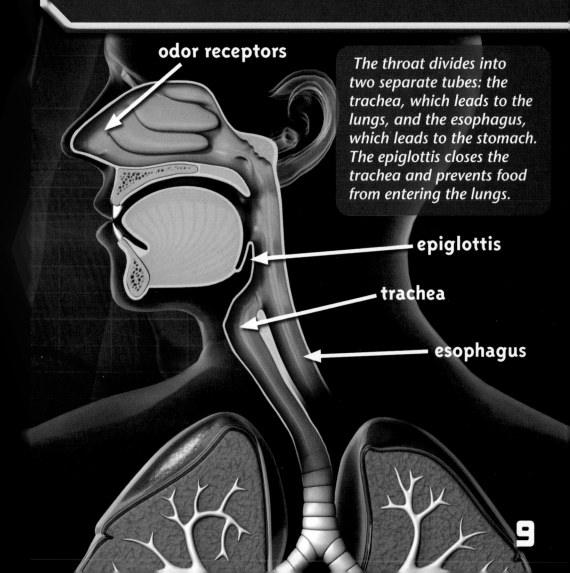

odor receptors

The throat divides into two separate tubes: the trachea, which leads to the lungs, and the esophagus, which leads to the stomach. The epiglottis closes the trachea and prevents food from entering the lungs.

epiglottis

trachea

esophagus

The Larynx

The trachea is a tube that's about as wide as a finger. It leads from the throat to the middle of the chest. To prevent this hollow tube from collapsing, it's held open by cartilage rings. Near the top of the trachea, just below the epiglottis, is a special ring of cartilage known as the larynx, which contains the vocal cords.

During normal breathing, the vocal cords are relaxed and held open so air may pass through them. When we speak, the cords tighten and vibrate, producing sounds. The more closely the cords are drawn together, the higher the pitch of the sound they make. The sound is further changed by how our lips and tongue are shaped while air escapes through our mouth.

IN THE FLESH

Adult men tend to have a larger larynx than women, which creates a deeper voice. A larger larynx results in a laryngeal prominence, or "Adam's apple."

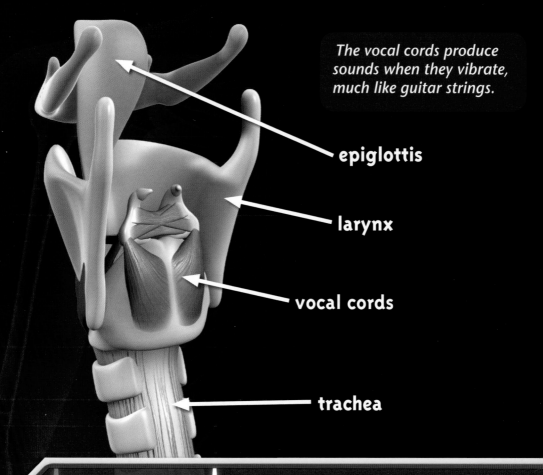

The vocal cords produce sounds when they vibrate, much like guitar strings.

epiglottis

larynx

vocal cords

trachea

CHOKING

Although the epiglottis closes the trachea when we swallow, food particles sometimes enter the trachea and block air from flowing. This is called choking. Choking can be deadly when the victim can't get enough air. Some people hit the choking victim on the back to try to knock the food out. However, this can make the food go deeper into the lungs. Instead, a method called the Heimlich maneuver uses air in the victim's lungs to force the food up and out of the trachea.

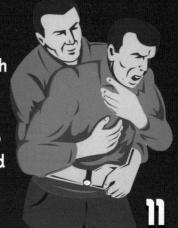

The trachea ends in the middle of the chest and divides into two branches, one for each lung. Each branch, or bronchus, enters a lung and divides into smaller tubes, called bronchioles. Each bronchiole divides into branches that become smaller and smaller until they're thinner than a human hair.

At the very end of each tiny bronchiole are extremely tiny sacs called alveoli. The walls of alveoli are so thin that oxygen can pass through them and flow into the nearby **capillaries**, beginning its journey through the circulatory system. Likewise, carbon dioxide in the capillaries flows through the alveoli walls to enter the lungs so it can be exhaled.

IN THE FLESH

An average adult has about 500 million alveoli. If you could stretch them out flat, they would cover a tennis court!

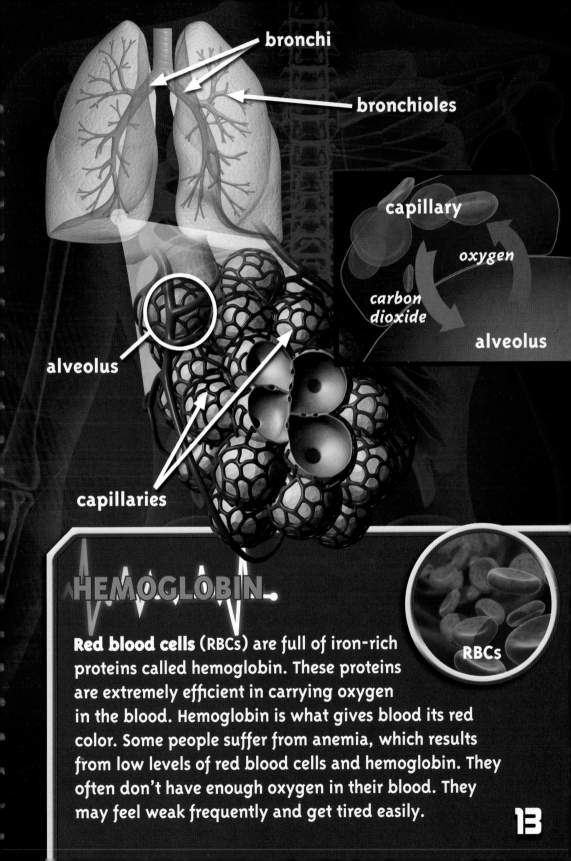

bronchi

bronchioles

capillary

oxygen

carbon
dioxide

alveolus

alveolus

capillaries

HEMOGLOBIN

Red blood cells (RBCs) are full of iron-rich proteins called hemoglobin. These proteins are extremely efficient in carrying oxygen in the blood. Hemoglobin is what gives blood its red color. Some people suffer from anemia, which results from low levels of red blood cells and hemoglobin. They often don't have enough oxygen in their blood. They may feel weak frequently and get tired easily.

RBCs

13

Breathing

So far, we've learned about the passageways connecting the alveoli to the outside air. But what makes air move into and out of our lungs?

When we breathe, we're changing the size of our lungs by contracting and relaxing the muscles in our rib cage and our diaphragm. The diaphragm is a sheet of muscles stretching across the inside of our body just below the lungs. When we inhale, our diaphragm contracts, which stretches the lungs down. At the same time, the muscles of the rib cage contract, which stretches the lungs wider. These actions result in the lungs getting bigger, and air is sucked into them. When we exhale, we relax the diaphragm and the muscles of the rib cage. This squeezes the lungs, which forces air out.

IN THE FLESH

People who live in mountainous places, where there are lower amounts of oxygen, have more red blood cells and hemoglobin to help carry oxygen in their blood.

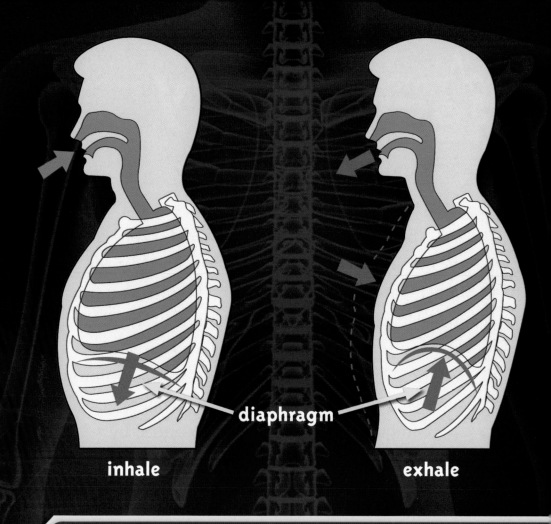

diaphragm

inhale

exhale

THE BRAIN STEM

There's a specialized area of the brain, called the brain stem, that controls many of the body's automatic functions. These include the beating of the heart and breathing. Special sensors in the body, called chemoreceptors, monitor the levels of oxygen and carbon dioxide. If the chemoreceptors sense that more oxygen is needed—for example, when we exercise—the brain stem signals the diaphragm to contract more quickly.

Respiratory Infections

Because the respiratory system is exposed to the outside environment, it's in constant danger of being **infected** by **viruses** and bacteria that can make us ill. The common cold is one of the most frequent human illnesses. Cold viruses attack and kill the cells in our nasal passages, causing symptoms such as runny nose, sore throat, and coughing.

Influenza, or "the flu," is also caused by viruses, but it can be more serious. Many of us recover from influenza within a week. However, it can be deadly for people who have weak **immune systems**, such as the elderly or very young babies. Doctors may recommend influenza vaccines for people who spend time with these at-risk people.

IN THE FLESH

There are no cures for colds and the flu, but we can prevent them from spreading by washing our hands after coughing and sneezing and before eating.

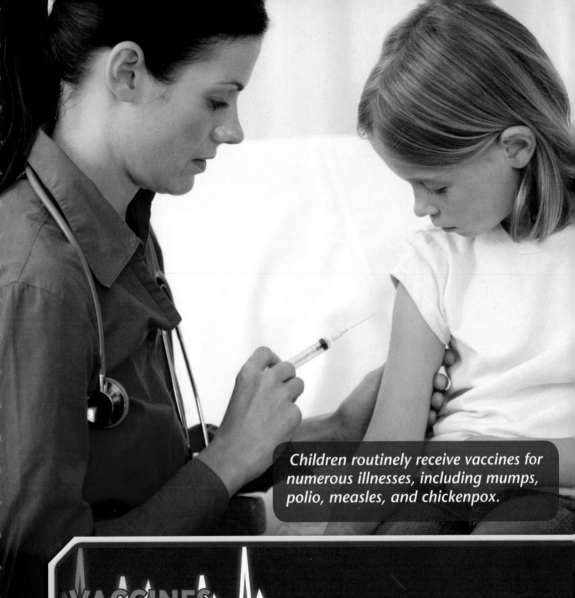

Children routinely receive vaccines for numerous illnesses, including mumps, polio, measles, and chickenpox.

VACCINES

Vaccines (sometimes called "shots") can sound scary, but they save lives! When you get a vaccine shot, a tiny amount of a dead or weakened virus or bacteria enters your body. These germs can't hurt you, but they do prompt your body to build a defense. Then, when your body is exposed to the strong, living germ, it's ready to fight. You won't get sick, and you won't spread the disease to anyone else!

Pneumonia is a serious infection of the lungs. It can be caused by viruses, bacteria, or funguses. While these germs are in the lungs, they damage the thin, delicate walls of the bronchioles and alveoli. When this happens, those parts can no longer supply oxygen to the blood. In addition, the thin walls of the alveoli allow these germs to enter the bloodstream, which spreads them throughout the body.

Without treatment, pneumonia will worsen. The lack of oxygen can become life threatening. **Antibiotics** and other medications can help fight the infection and help the patient breathe better. In some cases, the patient may need to be admitted to a hospital, where they're given higher amounts of oxygen until their lung function improves.

IN THE FLESH

While breathing higher amounts of oxygen can help you while you're sick, breathing 100 percent oxygen for too long may actually damage your lungs.

Some cases of pneumonia can be treated at home. Serious cases require the constant attention of trained medical professionals in a hospital.

KEEPING YOUR LUNGS CLEAN

When you inhale, you breathe in many tiny particles, including dust, pollen from plants, and bacteria. Alveoli contain specialized cells called macrophages, which is Greek for "big eaters." The macrophages do exactly what their name suggests: they literally eat all the bacteria, dust, and other particles they can find in the alveoli. This helps keep the lungs clean and healthy.

macrophage

19

Asthma

About one in 10 children suffer from asthma. During an asthma attack, the bronchi in the lungs begin to swell, squeezing the space inside them so that less air can pass through. Asthmatics must work their breathing muscles extra hard to keep air moving into and out of the lungs. There's always a danger that an attack lasts so long that the patient becomes too tired to breathe. Sadly, about nine people in the United States die every day from asthma.

Fortunately, there are good medications available to both treat and prevent asthma attacks. Albuterol is an inhaled medication that quickly widens the bronchi walls. Other daily medications are used to help prevent bronchial swelling in the first place.

Quick-acting medications, such as an albuterol inhaler, can help expand the bronchi and make it easier to breathe again.

ASTHMA TRIGGERS

In the majority of asthma cases, the swelling of the bronchi is triggered by some external factor. In many cases, it may be cigarette smoke, dust, pet dander, pollen, or cold air. In some cases, the asthma attack occurs when the person has an infection. It's very important that asthmatics and their families and friends do their best to avoid these triggers to help prevent attacks.

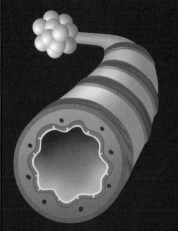

| normal airway | asthmatic airway | airway during asthma attack |

IN THE FLESH

Asthmatics often make a "wheezing" sound when they exhale as they push air through the narrower bronchi.

Other Lung Diseases

Emphysema (sometimes referred to as chronic obstructive **pulmonary** disease, or COPD) is a disease in which the alveoli become permanently damaged and scarred. Air exchange becomes extremely limited, and patients are short of breath all the time. Emphysema is a progressive disease, which means patients usually get sicker, not better.

More people die from lung cancer than any other type of cancer. Cancer occurs when cells of the body grow too quickly and don't work the way they should. Breathing becomes difficult for people with lung cancer. The cancer cells often spread to other organs as well. Although there are some treatments, especially when the disease is discovered early, many people still die.

IN THE FLESH

While smoking has been proven to cause most lung cancers, some people who never smoked still develop this terrible disease.

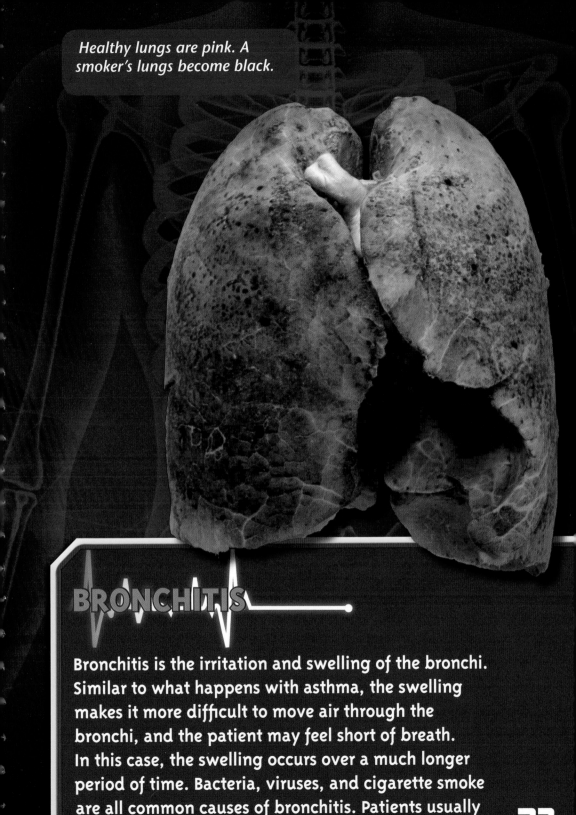

Healthy lungs are pink. A smoker's lungs become black.

BRONCHITIS

Bronchitis is the irritation and swelling of the bronchi. Similar to what happens with asthma, the swelling makes it more difficult to move air through the bronchi, and the patient may feel short of breath. In this case, the swelling occurs over a much longer period of time. Bacteria, viruses, and cigarette smoke are all common causes of bronchitis. Patients usually have a **productive cough** that can last for weeks.

Diagnosing Lung Diseases

The first thing a doctor does to diagnose, or identify, a patient's lung problems is to ask questions, such as: When did the problems start? Does anyone in your family have the same problem? Do you smoke?

Next, the doctor listens to the patient's chest with a **stethoscope** to make sure air is moving in all areas of the lungs. The doctor also listens for extra sounds, such as the "wheezing" usually heard in asthma or the "crackling" sometimes heard in pneumonia. The doctor may also check other parts of the body for signs of disease, including the back of the throat, nasal passages, ears, and even the skin.

IN THE FLESH

New machines called pulse oximeters use light, usually shining on the patient's finger, to quickly and painlessly measure how much oxygen is in the patient's blood.

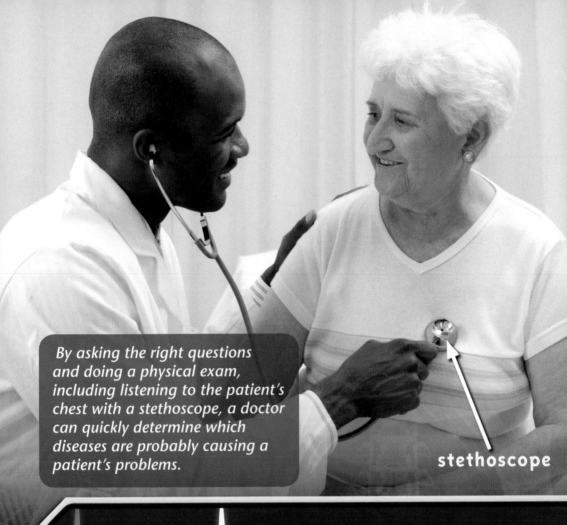

By asking the right questions and doing a physical exam, including listening to the patient's chest with a stethoscope, a doctor can quickly determine which diseases are probably causing a patient's problems.

stethoscope

THE ABCs

When seeing very sick patients with multiple problems, doctors think "ABC" to remind themselves of the most important problems to fix first. They first make sure the patient's **a**irway is open and able to transport air into the lungs. Next, doctors make sure the patient is **b**reathing. Finally, they make sure the patient's heart is **c**irculating blood (and oxygen) throughout the body. All three must be fixed before doctors worry about the patient's other problems.

Depending on the doctor's suspicions about which disease a patient may have, an X-ray may be requested. During an X-ray, energy passes through a person's body and onto special film. Solid structures in the chest, such as the ribs and heart, block some of this energy, while the lungs, because they're empty except for air, don't. Thus, the film can show physicians what the inside of a patient's chest looks like.

Like an X-ray, a CT scan uses energy passing through the body to take a picture of the inside. The CT scan takes a 3-dimensional picture, however, and shows many more details than an X-ray. On the other hand, it's slower than an X-ray and costs much more money.

IN THE FLESH

A bronchoscope is a long, thin tube with a camera on one end. Doctors can use it to view a patient's trachea, larynx, and bronchi.

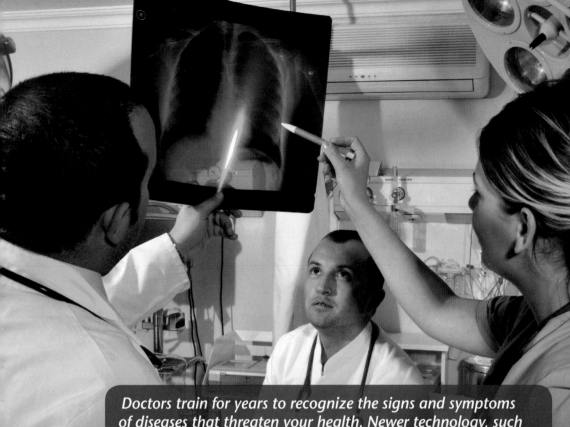

Doctors train for years to recognize the signs and symptoms of diseases that threaten your health. Newer technology, such as CT scans and bronchoscopes, gives doctors better tools to diagnose diseases more quickly and accurately.

PULMONARY FUNCTION TEST

X-rays and CT images show how the lungs appear. Pulmonary function tests (PFTs) are designed to measure how well the lungs work. Patients breathe into a machine that measures how much and how fast air is blown out. These tests are valuable for diagnosing asthma and emphysema. By comparing PFT results over time, doctors can determine if a patient is getting worse or if a new medication is helping.

Keeping Your Lungs Healthy

One of the most important health habits is to avoid cigarette smoke, including secondhand smoke. Medical science has proven that many deadly lung diseases are directly related to smoking.

Wearing special masks while working in dusty or dirty conditions can prevent harmful particles from being inhaled and damaging your lungs.

Make sure your home has a carbon monoxide detector. Carbon monoxide is a colorless, odorless gas that can bind to hemoglobin and prevent oxygen from being picked up and transported by RBCs. The lack of oxygen to the brain can result in death.

Just like you exercise your muscles to make them stronger, you should make your lungs stronger by doing aerobic exercises—those that make you breathe heavily—at least 1 hour every day. Jog, swim, or bike to keep your lungs in perfect shape!

CIGARETTE SMOKING AND
Your Health

LUNG CANCER

Chemicals in cigarette smoke can damage normal, healthy cells, turning them cancerous.

EMPHYSEMA

Smoke can scar alveolar walls, destroying their ability to allow oxygen and carbon dioxide to flow across.

PREGNANCY

Smoking during pregnancy has been shown to be very harmful, and in some cases deadly, for the baby.

BRONCHITIS

Constant irritation of smoke causes the bronchial walls to swell and produce mucus.

HEART

People who smoke are much more likely to have a heart attack than nonsmokers are.

ASTHMA

Cigarette smoke, even a tiny amount of secondhand smoke, can trigger a severe asthma attack.

MOUTH CANCER

Besides lung cancer, cigarette smoke has been proven to cause mouth and throat cancer.

HEMOGLOBIN

Cigarette smoke contains carbon monoxide, which can permanently bind to hemoglobin and prevent the blood from carrying healthy levels of oxygen.

Glossary

antibiotic: a drug that can kill bacteria in the body

bacteria: tiny, single-celled organisms. Some cause diseases in humans.

capillary: an extremely small blood vessel that can allow gases and nutrients to pass through its thin walls

cartilage: a tough but flexible tissue used to support some body structures, such as the throat, ear, and joints

cell membrane: the thin wall of a cell that separates it from the outside surroundings

circulatory system: the body system made up of the heart, blood vessels, and blood

immune system: the parts of the body that fight germs and keep it healthy

infect: to spread germs inside the body, causing illness

mucus: a thick, sticky fluid that helps trap dust and other particles

organism: a living thing

productive cough: type of cough in which a lot of mucus is brought up

pulmonary: having to do with the lungs

red blood cell: a specialized cell in the bloodstream that contains hemoglobin and helps transport oxygen

stethoscope: a special instrument used by medical professionals that allows them to hear very soft sounds coming from the chest

virus: a nonliving package of proteins and genes that can cause diseases in humans

For More Information

BOOKS

Parker, Victoria. *I Know Someone with Asthma*. Chicago, IL: Heinemann Library, 2011.

Simon, Seymour. *Lungs: Your Respiratory System*. New York, NY: Collins, 2007.

World Book. *The Respiratory System*. Chicago, IL: World Book, 2007.

WEBSITES

How to Do the Heimlich Maneuver
www.heimlichinstitute.com/page.php?id=34
Read instructions on how to perform the Heimlich maneuver on different types of people.

Respiratory System
health.howstuffworks.com/human-body/systems/respiratory
Check out many interesting articles, pictures, and videos explaining how the respiratory system (as well as other body systems) works.

Your Lungs & Respiratory System
kidshealth.org/kid/cancer_center/HTBW/lungs.html
This site is full of interactive quizzes and informative videos to help make learning about the respiratory system fun.

Index